Nature of the Vale

Poems of the Countryside and the Seasons

Bob Woodroofe

Greenwood Press

First Published 1993

This impression published 2019

Greenwood Press
38 Birch Avenue
Evesham
Worcs WR11 1YJ

http://greenwoodpress.co.uk

ISBN 978-0-9521165-0-9

Introduction

*Having been born & brought up in Evesham I obviously have
a special affinity for the Vale & it's countryside.*

*I have spent many happy hours walking the country lanes
& footpaths, enjoying the local flora & fauna, the landscape
& scenery & the people living in it.*

*This is my attempt to describe my feelings for the area & it's
wildlife. It has been influenced by two special literary figures
from the past. Richard Jefferies, the Natural History writer
from Coate in Wiltshire & John Clare, the 'Peasant Poet' from
Helpston in Northamptonshire.*

*How I found these two I don't know, but they have also proved
a constant source of inspiration to me. I hope they would
approve of my attempts to bring my feelings of the wonders
of Nature to a wider audience.*

Bob Woodroofe

Contents

Blossom Time

The Vale in spring, blossom time,
like a bride, so pure, so fine.
It wears its veil, decked out in white,
draped over the hills, what a sight.
Virgin white, tinted with fresh green
as leaves unfurl, complete the scene.
Wind blown snowstorms at a glance,
petals falling softly, down they dance
onto the bright green sward to lie,
like God's confetti from on high.
Gazing down from Hipton high,
Vale lit by sun from azure sky.
Black barn like upturned boat,
lost in sea of foam, afloat.
Fragile blooms holding future life,
frost cuts at them like a knife.
Full of promise of things to come,
sweet fruits of apple, pear and plum.
Each year we wait to see this sight,
nature so simple, yet pure delight.
Each year our hearts for blossom yearn,
may such a sight for ever return.

Another Lad of Evesham Vale

I'm just another lad brought up in Evesham's Vale,
of these fields and orchards I can tell a tale.
In summer sun and rain, winter snow and hail,
I'm just another lad brought up in Evesham's Vale.

Do you remember conkers high up in the trees,
green and spiny cases swinging in the breeze.
Anything that came to hand flew up in the air,
sticks, stones, bottles, cans, to bring us bounty fair.

Bake them in the oven, pickle them in brine,
drill them with a skewer, thread them on some twine.
Listen to that crack, nothing could be finer,
you never will believe me, once I had a twenty-niner.

Every birds nest in the neighbourhood we knew,
Wrens here, Goldfinch there, everything that flew.
Eggs kept in a shoebox, wrapped in cotton wool,
never could blow them with a pin, could you?

Then there were Sticklebacks, three spined and ten,
Loaches and Minnows, I remember when
we used to catch Daddyruffe by the score.
How come it's not like that round here anymore.

Bird scarers on a rope, went of with such a bang,
if you got too close, by god your ears rang.
Bows and arrows, lances, catapults, air gun,
all the scrapes we got into, but we had some fun.

We rode our bikes on Avon ice in nineteen sixty three,
it seemed as safe as houses, as far as we could see.
Picked frozen sprouts, heard each one crack as it left stem bare,
like a volley of gunshots in the silent winter air.

Swimming in the Avon by the old Common Road pool,
float down to the weir, mess about and play the fool.
Balance on the sill, lie in the foam and weed,
of thoughts of pollution we never took no heed.

Football every weekend , we must have been so fit,
cups and medals on the mantelpiece, we could play a bit.
Wingers, backs, half and full, inside forwards too,
we just played, isn't that what you're supposed to do.

Come August the plums were ready, ripe to pick,
Prolifics, Pershore eggs, Victorias, until they made you sick.
Baskets, ladders, boxes everywhere, you never saw such scenes,
finished with Bank Holiday, when we picked the Damazines.

Filling 2/6 deposit boxes, one by bloody one,
1/2 cwt. 56 lbs in each, until you reach the ton.
Down the Worcester road to pulp them into jam,
or off to Smedley's factory to put them in a can.

The apple orchard, Worcesters, juicy red and ripe,
A handful up the jumper as we went by each night.
They sent the diggers in, bulldozed it flat, now it's
Simon de Montfort drive, or something like that.

We had the odd pint, you know what lads are like,
had to dodge the copper, in case he threw us out.
Now they're gone, no longer can you drink in these,
Falcon, Woolpack, Rose and Crown, Cross Keys.

I'm just another lad brought up in Evesham's Vale,
of these fields and orchards I can tell a tale.
In summer sun and rain, winter snow and hail,
I'm just another lad brought up in Evesham's Vale

Surge of Spring

Days lengthen, sunshine once more,
Spring knocks gently on winter's door.
Throw it open wide, let the sun
pour in till spring is sprung.

Daffodils point green spears above the ground,
yellow trumpets open all around.
Shining Celandines star bright,
gazing upwards to new found light.

A Blackbird flutes from on high,
to each vantage point in turn he'll fly.
To pour forth his sweet song,
to find a mate before too long.

To fill with speckled eggs their nest,
kept warm by hen Blackbirds breast.
To hatch and feed their latest brood,
such a struggle to find them food.

Hear the croak of frog from the pond
as male and female claw and bond.
To lay a jellied mass of spawn,
the next frog generation is born.

Along the hedgerow, such a sight,
Blackthorn blossom shining bright,
so white and pure against branch so dark.
Hark, I think I hear a Lark,

Soaring upwards, singing, to the sun,
from dawn to dusk, till day is done.
rising high from green clothed field,
spears of wheat, promise of future yield.

Leafless Coltsfoot, a yellow disc glows,
as winter's snow melts and flows.
Slowly through warming ground it seeps,
feeds and swells streams, rivers deep.

Take all the cold and damp away,
welcome, welcome bright spring day.
Warm breeze, blue sky, green sward,
share these with me, you can't be bored.

Each year, each spring belies belief,
the surge of life, the green of leaf.
It never ceases to amaze me,
the glory of nature plain to see.

To John

Did you sit here, these hills and holes among,
Barnack, its hedges with wild Honeysuckle hung.
Pasque flowers nodding purple in the breeze,
Man Orchid armies marching towards the trees.

Sun still shines down so warm and bright,
flowers still adorn that hedgerow bright.
Little trotty still bobs by slow flowing stream,
in it still floats the stately Bream.

When you lay in these flower strewn fields,
passing time as church bell pealed.
Your life so hard, did you shed a tear,
dreaming of Mary, whom you loved so dear.

Perhaps you sat on warm Summer's eve,
to hear the Nightingale sing before you leave.
To stroll home down the darkening lane,
Damped by grasses, wet with Summer rain.

Your verses so much more alive than these,
full of flowers, birds, sky and breeze.
If only I could have tried to make you see
the pleasure your words have given to me.

You and I so many years apart,
the same thoughts from deep within the heart.
May lifes cares and troubles one day cease,
thank you for bringing me such peace.

Summer Swallow

Just like a summer swallow into my life you flew,
with you I soared in skies so blue.
But I should have known sweet natures ways,
that you only stay for summer days.
You brought me sunshine, warmth and love,
the sun shone from blue skies up above.
But I should have known that you would fly away,
that leave you had to, one grey autumn day.
Your memory so precious, I treasure dear,
now you are gone, chill winter's here.
Rain slashes cold against life's window pane,
I long for summer to return once again.
I hope that one bright spring day
that you will return to me to stay
and that I too can fly with you
in summer, winter, all year through.

Man on the Hill

Climbing up his presence you can feel,
once there, you almost want to kneel.
He's still there, the man on the hill,
his thoughts and dreams standing still.
Close to the sky, crowned by its forts,
there he lay and dreamt his thoughts,
gazed down upon his beloved Coate,
mind so full of Nature as he wrote.
So much I feel and think but cannot say,
he weaves into his words, in only his way.
Natures beauty, love and peace,
her wonders amaze, they never cease
to give me solace, when I'm in pain,
to make me whole, refreshed again.
Your fine words, in them I've found,
like you on grassy burial mound.
Something I thought I'd never find,
happiness, contentment, peace of mind.
Long may I feel and see as you
the beauty of nature through and through.
Read your flowing thoughts and words,
describing magic of flowers and birds.
May I always feel your presence there,
from Liddingtons top, high in the air.
Gazing up at the blue azure, that meant so much,
thrilling to skylarks song, you can almost touch
your presence, your words, I hear them still,
You'll always be there, the man on the hill.

Summer with you

I have the memory, long may it last,
may it never dim, never pass.
Please let it always be the same,
you, me, summer fields, always remain.
As we walk sweet summer through,
hand in hand, just me and you.
Cross flowered fields warmed by suns heat,
launching butterflies with our feet.
Bright blue Scabious, purple Knapweed,
food for our thoughts, just what we need.
Blue skies, white clouds, warm breeze,
what more can we ask but these.
Ripening fields of grain, glowing burnished gold,
what future is there, what does it hold.
Things change, times change and so do we,
they have to, we do to, it has to be.
Summer's over, past its best,
will our love stand the test.
Will it fall withered, like the leaves
of autumn from the trees.
Will it die from winter's cold,
have we enough in store to hold.
To last till summer comes once more,
to start again sweet nature's tour
of field and hedgerow shining bright,
under summer suns warmth and light.
Blue skies, white clouds, warm breeze,
what more can I ask but these, and you.

Avon Evening

By this river I have come to walk and rest,
to one of the places I know best.
I know here that I can find
tranquillity and peace of mind.

The evening sun catches the ripples as they die,
as Shakespeare's Avon slips gently by.
Rings made by a Mallard family,
as they paddle quietly away from me.

The distant hum of as they speed by,
in such a rush, I don't know why.
The pace seems quieter here, like the stream,
the water flows so fresh, so clean.

The cows breathe heavy, mist leaves their faces
as they squelch down to their drinking places.
Clumsily they chew their cud
as they struggle through the clinging mud.

Jet vapours trail across the sky
as Heron slowly flapping by
issues his harsh 'krank' on silent wings,
flies home to dream of fish and things.

Arrowhead stands sharp and green,
its little white flowers seem to gleam.
Purple Water mint that smells so sweet
when it's trodden by your feet.

An Alder stands with roots washed bare,
hidden beneath, a Water Vole's there,
gnawing loudly on stem of reed,
can't seem to satisfy its greed.

A Moorhen skulks among the flags and reeds,
she quietly clucks, helps her brood to feed.
sending ripple rings across the stream,
the wavelets lit by golden beams.

The Swallow still twitters overhead,
soon he will be gone to bed.
Soon be gone to far of lands
across the sea and distant sands.

The Reedmace stands like sentinel on high,
silhouetted against the sky.
Flowering rush, so pretty, so pink,
edges the pool where the dark cows drink.

The clouds are lit up pink as ducks flight by,
arrowing their way across the sky.
Forget-me-not winks blue from the lush green reeds,
such a mass of tangled water weeds.

A Pigeon clatters noisily from a tree,
shattering the peace and tranquillity.
A feather drifts down to the floor,
quiet and calm descends once more.

The water seems so pure and clean,
but underneath what lurks unseen.
What hidden things dissolved within,
birds and animals death to bring.

Where is the Kingfisher that used to flash
brightly cross the stream and then to splash
in the shallows for the little fish
to feed it's young a supper dish.

A fish rises, another fly meets its fate,
silently the Angler waits.
Hunched over rod, waiting for a bite,
straining his eyes in the failing light.

Waiting for a Chub, perhaps a Bream,
in this slow, deep meandering stream.
To seize his bait, pull his line tight,
don't give up without a fight.

Tansy buttons glow yellow in a clump,
standing upright by an old tree stump.
Thistles and nettles by the score,
Ragwort, Ox-eye daisy and many more.

This constant stream of water flowing past,
down to the Severn and the sea at last.
How many thousand gallons, how many miles,
as through the meadows it slowly files.

The Rooks caw loudly as they fly,
trailing home across the sky.
To roost in the wood upon the hill,
soon to be silent and so still.

The rocks that guard this weirpool round,
where did they come from, where were they found.
Gravel strewn with shells that glint pearl bright,
picked out by the suns fast fading light.

What huge river brought them down,
scattered them this weir around.
How far have they travelled from up the stream,
what great forces washed them down unseen.

A massive trunk, washed from who knows where,
crowns the weir, stands gaunt and seems to stare.
Waiting for winter's flood to carry it down,
carry it closer to Evesham town.

Gnats and midges dance across the sky,
moths and bats go flitting by,
such a wealth of life and death,
breathe it in with every breath.

A late boat chugs slowly up the stream,
lighting the river with its beam.
Loosestrife flowers purple bright,
picked out in the flashing light.

A house light winks on and beckons on the hill,
the river air is cold and chill.
Mist lies wreathed across field and stream,
above heads of grasses nodding green.

Hear the muffled roar of distant weir,
where the water pours so pure and clear.
Where it foams and sparkles in the light,
as sun sinks down and it is night.

Darkness falls, descends slowly down,
the lights come up in Evesham town.
A Little Owl screeches from opposite bank,
the dew on the grass is cold and dank.

As I slowly climb the hill, all is peaceful, all is still,
The air gets warmer, lifts the chill.
It seems to rise from the earth beneath my feet,
It welcomes you, smells so sweet.

As the river you slowly leave behind,
It seems to have brought you peace of mind.
What more can you do, what more can you say,
at the end of a perfect August day.

Windmill Day

Facing west across the Vale,
shrouded over with ghostly veil.
Drifting mist rolls over the river,
lit by morning suns first glimmer.

On the bank above the road,
diggings visible for all to behold.
Badger returns along well beaten trail,
nights wandering done cross hill and vale.

Snuffs morning air, nose held on high,
strange scents abroad, poised ready to fly.
home to his set to spend the day
in cosy bedding, with cubs to play.

The rising sun warms the chill air,
a breeze springs up below somewhere.
Clearing the mist slowly away,
lighting fields of glass with the day.

Grass glistening with damp dew,
clear morning sky, what a view
over the Vale to Malvern and beyond.
It's home to me, of which I'm fond.

There is always a wind on the hill,
always moving, never still.
Sometimes a breeze, often a gale,
Kestrels on outstretched pinions sail

above the sunbleached tufts of grass
that allows their prey to pass
undetected from other's eyes,
except those gazing down from autumn skies.

Buckthorn with its branches berry lined,
waiting for Brimstone butterfly to find.
After its wandering along hedgerow,
lay its eggs, next generation to grow.

Dry nodding Scabious and Knapweed heads
raised above grasses sharp edged beds.
Their nectar once did butterflies sustain,
now left to wind to spread the seeds again.

Gnarled Hawthorns defiantly stand,
bent by the winds strong shaping hand.
Stark outlined against sunsets glow,
reflecting red off Avon below.

The sun sinks as the sky shuts its door,
quiet evening comes to the hill once more.
Night slowly falls as darkness descends,
another Windmill day is at an end.

Malvern Memories

To these hills I come to rest,
gaze out over the Vale that I know best.
Clear my mind of everyday worry,
still life's crazy pace and hurry.

View some of Nature's store of treasure,
stop and watch with love and pleasure.
Recharge the heart and soothe the mind,
peace and solitude you can find.

What forces must have caused you to rise,
crumpled from Earth's crust upwards to the skies.
Ancient rocks from deep within the core,
one hundred million years old or more.

Beyond comprehension, such a time span,
stretching back to time before life began.
Rocks of crystal form your backbone,
Feldspar, Quartz, Granite hard stone.

Such a view from way up high,
seems you're closer to God and sky.
Bredon stands out rounded and clear,
another place that I hold dear.

You can see seven Counties on a clear day,
spread in the distance in every way.
Crossing your ridge, west from the river vales,
It's Hereford, but it feels like Wales.

Gaze down to the Commons from on high,
shimmering lake in your Golden Valley lie.
Sheep on your grasses contentedly graze,
hazy scene of warm summer days.

Twin beacons of two counties that you separate,
were fires lit to warn or celebrate
the passing of some milestone in our history,
warn of the Armada or some famous victory.

Did Elgar walk along your crests,
composing his music that you impressed
into his mind with your fine view,
English landscape, pure and true.

Did Druids come, sunrise to seek
on your hilltop fort so bare and bleak.
Toiling up your paths so worn,
just to view midsummer dawn.

At St. Anne's and Holy well too,
from rock fissures the water seeps through.
Spring water so pure and clear,
flows from the hill all the year.

Gullet lake, cold, clear and deep,
towered over by cliff so steep.
Quarried by Man's greedy hand,
gouging holes out of the land.

High Brown Fritillaries on fine Spring day,
quarter bracken hillside on Violets to lay.
Grayling lie, wings pressed to stony ground,
so camouflaged, they can't be found.

The Adder, zigzag skin newly bright,
coils and basks in the warm sunlight,
In shady woods, bells in endless sheets
colour spring blue around your feet.

Green, gold, purple, deep blue,
colours change as sun sets over you.
Your peaks picked out in varied hue,
each and every day a different view.

May I long walk your well worn tracks,
winding over your great humpbacks.
Rest on your summits, hear Priory bells ring,
soak up the peace that you bring.

To me and I hope to everyone,
in winter cold or summer sun,
forever in my heart defined,
memories of a special kind.

Poppy

You are the sweet Poppy in my life,
the splash of colour that brightens the strife.
The one that stands out in lifes sea of gold,
that sea looks so lovely, but it's oh so cold.

Without you, bright and cheery like the colour red,
life seems so dreary, dull and dead.
I want so much to be there with you.
I love you so much, if only you could too.

But deep in my heart, I cannot lie,
like the Poppy, I saw your love fade and die.
Thoughts and dreams vanish, tell me why,
why does it hurt so much, make me cry.

I am lost in that sea of gold,
my heart, my body, aches for you to hold.
Like a lifeboat on lifes cruel sea,
I know that once you rescued me.

I don't want to be cast adrift once more,
I'm tired of swimming for the shore.
I want to find an island on this sea,
settle down, feel secure, just you and me.

Colour that golden sea with splashes of red,
dream bright poppies each time we go to bed.
Warm summer days filled with golden grain,
shut out the heartache and the pain.

And you, my bright fragile red flower,
you give me so much hope, strength, so much power.
To want to carry on, to live life through,
I owe so much, all this to you.

Lone Tree

A tree stands gaunt, alone, in field so green,
brown, withered and dry, not a leaf to be seen.
You were once mighty Ulmus, majestic Elm,
lord of the fields, king of your realm.

Why did you die, what caused you to wither,
did beetle under your bark slink and slither,
eat your heart away, slow lingering death,
slowly strangled you lost your last breath.

You stand so complete, your outline
must have looked majestic in its prime.
You seem so proud, once so free,
now only firewood, destined to be.

Standing here, how long have you been,
how many of life's seasons have you seen.
Growing slowly upwards to the sky,
seeing all as time went by.

To each and all you gave shelter and food,
a myriad of insects your bark and leaf chewed.
The birds in your arms their nests once made,
your spreading branches the cattle gave shade.

Do you remember the boys that used to grope
among your branches, to swing on a rope.
Climb up high to see the view,
build a tree house inside of you.

Did White Letter Hairstreaks flight round your top,
caterpillars your leaves no more to crop.
They too, like you, died or flew away
to find other trees on which to lay.

Age aching limbs that have seen such time,
carried huge weight of leaf and sap in their prime.
Now the wind has stripped you like a knife,
yet you are complete, except leaves, except life.

Leaves no longer green, your twigs are numb,
they have all fallen, final autumn has come.
The wind does not rustle them any more,
just creaks your branches, rattles deaths door.

Don't let them fell you with frantic buzzing saw,
sharp, so brutal, savaged to the floor.
You took so many years to grow,
please let the world destroy you slow.

Let the elements gently eat you away,
wind, rain and sun you gracefully decay.
Falling branch by bough with dignity and pride,
into the earth from whence you came, reside.

Pale fingers of fungi creep through your heart
extracting all the goodness before you depart.
Fruiting bodies mushroom as you die,
pouring spores into the sky.

Life goes on without you, less one tree,
does it really matter, it does to me.
Nature's eternal cycle, going round and round
returning you once more into the ground.

I will return one day to see your fate,
rooted to the spot you can but wait
to see how time at its own pace
will reduce you to dust, lost without trace.

I hope one day from deep within the soil,
from a root still alive a sucker will toil
up to the light and form a fine tree,
just as magnificent as you used to be.

Autumn Harvest

Red gold colours tint the trees,
leaves are falling, fluttering in the breeze,
they fall in heaps upon the floor,
drift so deep by cottage door.

Summer is over, autumn is born,
the fields are all so neatly shorn,
nature's larder is filled once more,
nuts and berries by the score.

All summer's goodness stored away,
to last until the first spring day.
Food for Fieldfares, Redwings too,
to last them all the Winter through.

Cobwebs glisten with the dew
as the morning sun creeps slowly through
the mist that seems to hang from every tree,
the distant hills you can hardly see.

The grass is yellow, dry to the touch,
the sun's still warm, but not as much.
The air is cooler than before,
time to wrap up warm and close the door.

Elderberries hang black on every bush,
leaves yellowed with the first blush
of autumn's shades and hue.
Nights draw in, winter's due.

A bright yellow Brimstone flutters by,
to find a winter's home it's time to try.
To sleep peacefully and to dream
of Buckthorn shoots so fresh and green.

The berries on the hedgerow shining bright,
picked out by the pale sunlight.
Warnings of hard times to be,
but nature will survive you'll see.

Come next spring all will be revealed,
from under winter's cloak concealed.
As the sun opens next seasons door,
nature's pulse will rise anew once more.

Ancient Days

Windmill hill, today so cold and wet,
looks like so much pasture land and yet
faint impressions of ditch and bank
into the hillside grass have sank.

An Enclosure, this hill once occupied,
a Causewayed settlement, long since died.
Round Barrows, bowls upturned against the sky,
within our ancestors left to die.

Look around, pick out the sign,
tree marked Barrows on the skyline.
Silbury Hill rises, attracts the gaze,
faintly visible through the haze.

Avebury, such a spectacle, such a sight,
awesome by day, mystical by night.
Such massive stones, ditch so deep,
encircled by the bank so steep.

How much sweat and strain did it take
to lever each stone into place.
Rising upwards, pointing to the skies,
each ancient Sarsen, here it lies.

The circles within, the Cove as well,
each has its meaning, none can tell
what ancient ceremony took place here,
we can guess, but it's not clear.

The wind chills cold as up we climb
this long straight path to where we find
this Long Barrow, so very old,
West Kennet, sombre, dark and cold.

The stone slabs guard the entrance round
as if protecting the burial mound.
Who is interred here, warrior or chief,
laid to rest with ancient grief.

So much work and toil to create
this monument to someone's fate.
This reverence for dead and death
for us to view with bated breath.

Such a hill, it belies belief,
standing out, just like a reef.
Silbury, artificial man made mound
so steeply rising from the ground.

Such a prodigious feat by man and beast,
twelve million cubic feet of chalk at least.
What did they see, nearer the sky,
from this vantage point on high.

These settlements, burials, the people's ways,
we know so little of these ancient days.
We can but look and continue to dream
of what their lives must have been.

Bleak Winter

Bleak winter is here, frost rimes the trees,
temperatures falling, feel the air freeze.
In its icy grasp winter does hold
us all for months, dark and cold.

November fog, thick and icy cold,
closes in around you, seems to hold
you enfolded in it's ghostly hand,
lost and stranded in mist covered land.

The feeble sun peers through the mist
Icicles with its pale gleam kissed
glitter coldly from where not long ago
Swallows used to nest, fly to and fro.

Snow falls, the wonder of each magic flake,
pure white crystals, so beautifully ornate.
Snow accumulates, bears down tree branches,
cold winter gusts launch small avalanches.

Landmarks all hidden, don't know which way to go,
crisp crunchy softness as you tread the snow.
White world of drifts shaped by winters hand,
wandering entranced in this eerie wonderland.

Now there is stillness, no sound of birds,
cold so cruel you can't describe in words.
Breath mists the air as it leaves faces,
wind fills footprints, leaving no traces.

Moaning in chimney, the winter gale
rushes on its way, under full sail.
See how it drifts the falling snow,
doesn't seem to know which way to blow.

Christmas time, love, peace and giving,
happy families together, life for the living.
Full and content by warm fireside,
spare a thought for those outside.

Leafless tree outlined against cold grey sky,
whipped by freezing wind as it blasts by.
No shelter here for man or beast,
we long for the roaring wind to cease.

The birds clamour over berries blood red,
fuel to keep them warm,or else they're dead.
Little Robin with red splashed breast,
nowhere warm for him to rest.

Frost patterns crack on the window panes,
strange shapes, linked in frozen chains.
The pond is solid, gripped in winter's vice,
water frozen, plants entombed in ice.

Dress up warm before you go out
to snowball fight, hear the children shout.
Fingers numb with cold, noses cherry red,
wouldn't you rather be warm in your bed.

Build a snowman from cold slushy snow,
he seems to last forever, melts so slow.
Get the sledge out, down the slope slide,
just one more time, just one more ride.

This white world, bound in ice and snow,
how we long for it all to go.
Release its icy grip on our cold hearts,
feel the warmth as a new spring starts.

And yet as each winter passes by,
over ice hard ground the snow does lie.
Its pure whiteness seems to cleanse the earth,
Another fresh new year is given birth.

Three in a Million

Small brown bird floating way up high,
Skylark singing summer to blue vaulted sky.
Pouring forth your song from way up in the air,
how can we let such beauty become so rare.

Over silver meadows glinting in the watery light
the Lapwing in soaring exuberant flight,
calling 'peewit', swerving, falling from the skies,
we surely can't allow this glorious sight to die.

Did you ever see on misty moonlit night
the white Owl slip by in silent ghostly flight.
Where are the mice to eat, the barns in which to nest,
are we sure when we say that man knows what's best.

*Let us not forget from whence we came
The Earth is home to all of us
Let us treat it accordingly*

About the Author

*Born & bred & still living in the Vale of Evesham
Bob Woodroofe's poems appear in many poetry
magazines & are performed locally. Inspired by
the natural world, the landscape & local tradition
he attempts to bring the magic of nature & its
restorative & healing qualities to a wider audience.*